50 WAYS
TO
HELP SAVE
THE
BEES

THE COUNTRYMAN PRESS

A Division of W. W. Norton & Company

Independent Publishers Since 1923

50 WAYS
TO
HELP SAVE
THE
BEES

Sally
Coulthard

50 WAYS TO HELP SAVE THE BEES is intended to provide helpful and informative material on the subject matter covered, not as a substitute for professional advice where warranted. Please use common sense, particularly where children are concerned, and consult a physician before engaging in any of the activities described if you are sensitive, or have a known or suspected allergy, to bee stings. Neither the publisher nor the author can guarantee the accuracy and completeness of this book for all purposes or make any representation with respect to the outcome of any project or instruction described. Web addresses appearing in this book reflect existing links as of the date of first publication. No endorsement of or affiliation with any third party website should be inferred. Author and publisher are not responsible for any third-party product, service, service provider, or content (including any website, blog, information page, or otherwise). This book is sold without warranty of any kind, and none may be created or extended by sales representatives or written sales or promotional materials.

Copyright © 2019 by Sally Coulthard

First American Edition 2021
Originally published under the title *The Bee Bible: 50 Ways to Keep Bees Buzzing*

All rights reserved
Printed in the United States of America

For information about permission to reproduce selections from this book, write to Permissions, The Countryman Press, 500 Fifth Avenue, New York, NY 10110

For information about special discounts for bulk purchases, please contact W. W. Norton Special Sales at specialsales@wwnorton.com or 800-233-4830

Manufacturing by Versa Press
Production manager: Devon Zahn

The Countryman Press
www.countrymanpress.com

A division of W. W. Norton & Company, Inc.
500 Fifth Avenue, New York, NY 10110
www.wwnorton.com

978-1-68268-626-3 (pbk.)

10 9 8 7 6 5 4 3 2 1

CONTENTS

How doth the little busy bee
Improve each shining hour,
And gather honey all the day
From every shining flower!

How skilfully she builds her cell!
How neat she spreads the wax!
And labours hard to store it well
With the sweet food she makes.

– ISAAC WATTS,
'How Doth the Little Busy Bee'

INTRODUCTION

Bees have seen it all. They've watched mighty dinosaurs roam the Earth, kept buzzing through glacial ice age after ice age, and gone about their business as great civilisations rose and fell. Bees have bumbled along, silent witnesses to human evolution, our discovery of fire and the beginnings of agriculture, through centuries of rapid change and industrial growth.

They're quiet survivors, brilliant at adapting to ever-changing circumstances and new environments. Bees have colonised almost every corner of the planet – from the mountains of North America to the Himalayas, the Amazonian rainforest to the rolling hills of England – and yet, of the 100 million years since bees evolved from wasps, and went their pollen-preferring ways, now is perhaps the most challenging time of all.

Bees are in trouble and they need our support. So that's what this book is about. It's a call to action. It's a collection of positive things that we, as individuals, can do to help. Some are choices we can make as consumers. Others are changes we can make to our gardens or public green spaces. But there are also actions we can take that can influence government policy for the better. Working together as a collective, we can get things done.

Little things can make a big difference. Just ask a bee.

WHAT'S HAPPENING TO BEES?

It's a complex picture and one that's worth taking some time to unpick. Back in the late 1990s and early 2000s, many beekeepers across the world were noticing that their honey bees were dying in unprecedented numbers. Entire colonies were mysteriously wiped out, leaving hives empty and beekeepers (and the rest of the world) worried that honey bees were crashing towards mass extinction, a fate that would have desperate consequences for the world's ecosystem and food supply. It was headline-grabbing stuff.

No one was sure why so many honey bee colonies were dying – an event that became known as Colony Collapse Disorder (CCD). Subsequent research has shown that it was probably a number of factors, working in deadly harmony – a perfect storm of invasive varroa mites, habitat loss, low bee immunity caused by poor management of hives or overexposure to pesticides, and other interrelated factors.

The good news, however, is that the situation for managed honey bees – that is, bees kept by beekeepers – has improved. Numbers are slowly recovering and reported cases of CCD have dwindled. Even better, thanks to the concerted efforts of many beekeeping groups and media campaigns, beekeeping as a hobby has rocketed in popularity. In the United States, the "Save the Bees" slogan is printed on stickers and posters and bee-patterned clothes appear in stores across the country. Bees are definitely having a moment.

So why should we still be worried about them? The answer is twofold. The first reason is that, despite a surge of interest in beekeeping, there has still been an overall decline in honey bees over the past half-century. The second reason is that honey bees aren't the only bees that matter. In the US, for example, there are more than 4,000 species of native bees. These species fall within different categories. Many species are solitary, pollinating lone rangers who don't care for life in the hive. Other species fall under the broad category of bumblebee – but there are even different varieties of this familiar fat and fluffy bee.

Honey bees aren't the only bees that matter. In the US, there are more than 4,000 species of bees.

––––––––––

Over the past fifty years, these species numbers are shrinking, with some becoming extinct. In Europe, nearly one in ten species of wild bees faces extinction, and in the US about a quarter of all wild bees have disappeared in the past ten years alone. Pollinators of all kinds – bees, butterflies, moths and other bugs – are showing declines worldwide and although not all species are threatened (some are even improving their numbers), the overall picture is alarming.

WHY ARE BEES IMPORTANT?

The decline of bees is part of a much bigger picture. We like to think that we don't rely on the natural world for much – wildlife exists for many of us solely in the background, as a pretty backdrop to our busy lives, something to watch on television or visit at the weekend. And yet few of us realise just how dependent we are on wild organisms for our very survival. Agriculture and human health rely heavily on the unpaid work done by an entire ecosystem that's largely invisible – the worms and woodlice that create healthy soil for us to grow things in, the woodlands that pump fresh air into the environment, the wild birds that gobble up many of the pests that would otherwise ruin our crops and gardens.

Bees punch well above their weight when it comes to helping humans – keeping themselves busy, pollinating a vast array of our favourite foodstuffs. From almonds to coffee, strawberries to apples – at least **a third of all our food** is pollinated by bees and other creatures (not just crops, but also fruit, vegetables and the feeds given to meat and dairy animals). And while managed bees do some of this work, the lion's share is still done by wild insects.

If bees disappeared – wild or managed – the results would be catastrophic. In some places, the unthinkable has already happened; in Hanyuan, China, for example, the widespread use of pesticides has decimated the wild bee population, leaving pear farmers with the laborious task of pollinating fruit trees by hand. Other countries have been finding their own solutions – in the Netherlands, for  example, where half their 360 species of bees are threatened, scientists have developed a 'robo-bee', a tiny flying drone that will pollinate plants if bees aren't around to do it. Leaving aside the moral implications, replacing bees with either people or machines is not a long-term strategy, not least because of how economically unfeasible it would be on any large scale.

Instead of changing how we farm, some research is going into creating a 'super bee' capable of coping with the barrage of assaults

Agriculture and human health rely heavily on the unpaid work done by an entire ecosystem that's largely invisible

that modern life throws at it. It's still in its infancy but there is a plan to create a genetically modified bee that's resistant to both natural and human hazards, not least pesticides but also varroa and other diseases. It's a great idea on paper but many beekeepers worry about not only failing to tackle the root causes of bee decline but also the long-term effect of introducing a new, dominant, lab-designed bee on both traditional honey bee populations and wild species.

Beyond the relationship between bees and farming, about **90 per cent of wild plant species** depend, at least in part, on pollination by bees and other pollinating creatures. It's a rich, long-standing mutual relationship. A wide variety of plants – flowers and trees – can only exist if there is a wide variety of bees; bees come in all shapes and sizes, many with different tongue lengths and plant preferences. If we want our country-side to be filled with a glorious array of different plants, we need different types of bees to pollinate them. Equally, we can only support a wide range of bees if we leave them a varied enough range of plants to choose from.

And while lots of different animals are pollinators (including moths, flies, beetles, bats, hummingbirds and butterflies), bees are particularly good at it – the gold medal winners of the pollinator world. This is because both bee larvae and adults rely almost uniquely on pollen and nectar for their food. To get enough to eat, the number of visits bees make to flowers, as well as the distance travelled between flowering plants, is greater than any other kind of pollinating animal.

Interestingly, even plants that don't *need* bees to help them pollinate seem to benefit from the presence of bees. Much of the conversation about bees and other pollinating insects has focused on their relationship with insect-pollinated plants. And yet, we know from various studies that bees (and other insects) also visit wind-pollinated plants and self-pollinating plants (like strawberries). Some plants have evolved so they can be pollinated a number of different ways – a form of 'hedging their bets' in case one method fails or disappears. This has two important implications – one for humans and one for bees. The first is that studies are showing that some plants actually *grow better* if they are pollinated by bees rather than one of their alternative methods – experiments with strawberry plants, for example, showed that

Even plants that don't need bees to help them pollinate seem to benefit from the presence of bees

those pollinated by bees were redder, brighter, firmer and showed fewer deformities than those that were pollinated in other ways. They also had a shelf life twelve hours longer than non-insect-pollinated strawberries. This may not sound like much but it means strawberries remain fresh for longer, adding significantly to the value of the crop. Previous studies have shown similar findings for melons, cucumbers and a number of other fruits.

We can also use this information when it comes to planting with bees in mind. Traditionally, ways of helping bees have focused on insect-pollinated flowers, but we now know that bees can make use of a number of other plants, not least wind-pollinated trees, which can produce huge amounts of pollen, often when flowering plants are yet to bloom. So, if we want to help bees, for example, we can look beyond fruit trees or ornamental blossom and include other species such as oak, maple and willow.

ARE BEES IN TROUBLE?

One of the problems has been that it's tricky to pinpoint exactly what is harming bees. But understanding how bees operate gives us clues to what's going wrong.

The life of a bee is an industrious one. It takes a huge amount of energy, and brain power, to collect pollen and nectar. Bees need to navigate huge distances, remembering sources of food and how to get back home again. Bees' brains might be tiny but they can interpret different kinds of landscapes, flower species, shapes and patterns. Bees have been shown to be able to work out the shortest distances between objects, display both long- and short-term memory, communicate symbolically and demonstrate spatial awareness. Anything that interferes with these cognitive abilities has a devastating impact on bees. If a bee can't forage properly, find its way home or taste properly, it'll die. Equally, if its digestion is impaired or immunity compromised, a bee becomes more susceptible to illness. And this is the issue. A number of things we do, in the modern world, are interfering with bees' ability to function properly. No single thing is killing them off – it's more that a range of what are called *sub-lethal stressors* are weakening bees and affecting their behaviour.

Here are just a few of the things bees have to contend with:

HABITAT LOSS

Just like us, bees need a varied diet to thrive. No single pollen source contains all the vitamins, proteins and other goodies necessary for nutrition. Intensive monoculture agriculture, where one type of crop is grown on a large scale, reduces plant diversity. This, combined with a loss in natural habitat from increasing urbanisation, places nutritional stress on bees, who have to cope with a decrease in the quality and quantity of nectar and pollen available. Starvation leads to bee losses and poor colony health. The loss of uncultivated, natural habitat also creates issues for wild bees, who need places to nest and reproduce.

PESTICIDES/HERBICIDES

A number of widely used chemicals are making life difficult for bees. *Neonicotinoids* (which are sprayed onto crops such as wheat and barley to kill pests such as aphids) have been shown to cause a wide range of problems for bees, impacting their ability to navigate and reproduce. The European Union recently banned neonicotinoids for outdoor use in agriculture. Meanwhile, in the United States, the EPA banned 12 neonicotinoid pesticides in 2019, although some neonicotinoids still remain on the market. Nutritional stress has been shown to exacerbate the negative effect of neonicotinoids in bees. Similarly, a common weedkiller – *glyphosate* – in high doses seems to disrupt bees' digestive systems, making them more vulnerable to infection. It's a complicated issue – farmers are being asked to produce greater quantities of food, at ever cheaper prices, and scientific studies about which chemicals cause harm frequently contradict each other or bring up new evidence, with farmers often playing catch-up. Take *chlorothalonil*, for example, a fungicide that has been widely used since the mid-1960s. Farmers have been using this on barley, wheat and other crops for years, but it was only in 2017 that research finally discovered a link between *chlorothalonil* and bumblebee declines. The EU recently voted to ban it but it makes one wonder how many other pesticides and agricultural chemicals are unwittingly harming bees.

LIGHT POLLUTION

Street lights can throw the behaviour of nocturnal creatures into disarray. Some insects fly at night, dawn or dusk and studies have shown that artificial lighting interferes with their pollinating habits. If street lights drive away the night-time pollinators, it means less fruit and fewer plants overall, a change that then has a knock-on effect on daytime foraging bees. (There are also several species of mainly tropical bees – like the Central American sweat bee or the Indian carpenter bee – that have evolved to fly at night. These species may also be affected by night-time light pollution.)

CLIMATE CHANGE

A recent UN report revealed the potential effects of climate change on bees and other pollinators. It highlighted two specific problems: the first is that habitats where bees forage will change as the climate gets hotter – the balance of plants may alter with no guarantee that bees will be able to adapt; the second is the changing seasonal behaviour of different species. Thanks to warmer weather, and seasons arriving earlier, many wild bee species are emerging too soon. And while some flowering plants will also start to blossom earlier, there is a lag between the two. In other words, bees are waking up before any of their food sources are available to eat.

PESTS AND PATHOGENS

Bees, like any other animal, can get sick. Honey bees, because they live in colonies, are particularly susceptible to the rapid spread of infectious diseases; the honey bee hive is a crowded, warm environment, the perfect setting for pests and pathogens to exploit. Thankfully, honey bees are brilliant at keeping diseases at bay – over millions of years they have evolved various strategies and defence mechanisms to cope with potential attacks, from scrupulous hygiene and antibiotic propolis to undertaker bees to clear out the sick and dying. We are only just beginning to understand how sophisticated these methods are. Unfortunately, some parasitic diseases have hit hives hard in the past decades, undermining colonies already weakened by exposure to pesticides, lack of nutrition or a changeable climate. These parasites include:

- *nosema*, a parasitic fungus that causes dysentery
- *tracheal mite*, a parasite that shortens the lifespan of bees
- *varroa*, a mite that deforms wings and weakens the colony
- *bacteria* that cause a fatal disease known as foul brood.

BAD BEEKEEPING

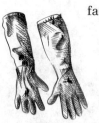

Following on from pests and pathogens, some of the issues facing honey bee hives are made worse or spread through poor management of colonies. Diseases can be spread through contaminated combs or hive equipment, for example, or by ignoring simple hygiene practices. Beekeeping associations recommend that beekeepers can reduce the impact of pests and diseases using apiary hygiene, regular brood comb changes, the right treatments, and ensuring that colonies are strong, fit and well-nourished to begin with.

DISEASE TRANSFER

Diseased honey bees can also affect wild populations, usually when they feed on the same flowers. One disease in the UK, for example, called *deformed wing virus*, is thought to have transferred from honey bees to wild bumblebees this way. The University of Cambridge's Zoology Department compared the transfer of these illnesses to 'germs passing between humans through a shared coffee cup'. Simply keeping more honey bees, therefore, is not the answer to declining bee populations. In fact, 'bad beekeeping' may be making things worse, not only by spreading pathogens but also by encouraging farmed bees to compete for pollen and nectar in an ever-diminishing natural world.

DIESEL EXHAUST FUMES

Traffic fumes, which contain toxic nitrogen oxide, are not only harmful to human health; exposure to diesel exhaust emissions has been shown to affect bees' ability to recognise different flower scents. Studies of polluted environments revealed that diesel fumes chemically alter almost half of the most common flower scents that bees use to find their food, confusing their sense of smell and making it difficult for them to forage.

FEAR OF BEES

Many people are scared of bees. One issue is that we lump all bees, wasps and other insects with similar colouration into the same category. And while a few species can be aggressive, most bees will only sting if seriously provoked and male bees have no sting at all. Bumblebees are not naturally aggressive.

Solitary bees rarely sting, and in most cases the sting is not particularly painful. And honey bees may sting but usually only if they're defending something – that is, their hive, which is why beekeepers wear suits. The most 'terrifying' of all bee spectacles – a honey bee swarm – is ironically a time when they are at their most docile and least likely to sting. And if we find a wild nest, we tend to panic and call in the exterminators.

Part of the issue may be a greater public awareness of extreme allergic reactions to bee stings. And while it's important not to dismiss the 2–5 per cent of people who develop severe allergies to bee stings, it's also important to note how *rare* deaths from bee stings are. Between 2008 and 2015, for example, in the US the number of deaths caused collectively by hornets, wasps *and* bees was 1.4 annual deaths per 10 million people. Pet dogs caused almost as many fatalities, at 0.8 deaths per 10 million people, and yet we have a completely different relationship with them. It's also interesting that, in the search for a cure for severe venom allergies, bee stings might provide the answer – experiments are showing that high doses of bee venom early in the year seem to block further reactions later in the season.

DIFFERENT KINDS OF BEES

Not all bees are the same. That's why we need different strategies to help different kinds of bees. They have very different lives – some are social and live in densely populated hives, others are solitary and spend their short lives alone. Some are semi-social, tolerating the company of a few other bees or sharing a few chores to lighten the load.

Worldwide there are about 20,000 different kinds of bee (9 types of honey bee, around 250 species of bumblebee, and the rest solitary bees). Some are as big as a thumb – like Wallace's giant bee of Indonesia. Others are tiny – like

No male bees can sting – they just don't have the right equipment

the Quasihesma bee of Australia, the males of which can be less than 2mm (0.08 inch) long. Some bees sting – such as the female honey bee. Many don't. In fact, 500 species of bees are classed as 'stingless'. And no male bees can sting – they just don't have the right equipment.

The way bees organise themselves varies hugely. Honey bees are at one end of the scale – living in huge 50,000-strong colonies consisting of one queen, thousands of female worker bees (who forage, make honey, clean and guard the hive), and a few hundred short-lived male drone bees whose sole job is to fertilise the queen. Honey bees in the wild live in nests they build in tree cavities or clumped under cliff edges, but for thousands of years humans have attempted to mimic the natural nest by building beehives. Designs have varied hugely – from ancient straw skep baskets, which often involved killing the bees to harvest the honey, to the latest flow hive, a honey bee house that lets you siphon off honey without disturbing the bees.

Bumblebees, on the other hand, live in much smaller groups – usually in colonies of between 50 and 500 in number. Many species of bumblebee like to make their nests underground, in dry spaces such as abandoned mouse nests. Others prefer life above ground, nesting in dead wood, holes in trees or long grass.

And then there's the solitary bee. The least recognised species in many ways, but the most numerous, solitary bees make up over 95 per cent of all bees. Some live underground, others like hollow plant stems, reeds or holes made by other insects. Some even like to nest in old snail shells or abandoned bird boxes. Solitary bees don't live in colonies – the female lays her eggs in the nest, leaves a little food behind, seals up the compartment and buzzes off. That's as far as the childcare goes. The male larvae will often hatch first, ready to mate when the females finally emerge.

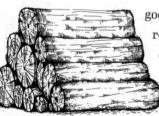

The fact that most bees don't live in a hive, and instead choose to make their homes in long grass, piles of wood, banks of earth and other marginal places, explains why native populations struggle if they can't find enough wild areas. Loss of natural habitat doesn't just affect the availability of flowering plants, it also means they have nowhere to nest and raise new bees.

WHAT BEES EAT

When you see bees buzzing around outside, they're most likely looking for nectar and pollen. Nectar contains sugar and pollen is packed full of protein, so the bees can use these two foods to feed not only themselves but also their young and other members of the colony if they live in a hive. Honey is made by honey bees from nectar, to see them through the winter, when there's no other food about and it's too cold to fly. In fact, honey is so good as a winter 'store cupboard' food source for bees that it can last almost indefinitely without going off; when archaeologists were excavating ancient Egyptian tombs, they found jars of 3,000-year-old honey that were still perfectly edible.

Solitary bees, on the other hand, don't make honey and bumblebees only make tiny amounts of a honey-like substance, which they eat themselves. This is because neither solitary bees nor bumblebees are awake during winter – bumblebees either die off or, if it's a queen bumblebee, she'll hibernate. Most solitary bee adults also die off before winter comes, leaving young pupae to grow in the nest over the cold months; the new bees emerge in the spring or summer.

The relationship between bees and plants is incredibly complex; in fact, we're only just beginning to understand how nuanced it is. Both bees and insect-pollinated plants have evolved to benefit each other – over the millions of years that they have depended on each other, bees have developed in different ways to become more effective pollinators, and plants have evolved to become more and more attractive to certain bees.

Some plants, for example, 'lace' their nectar with other chemicals, such as caffeine or nicotine, to make them more attractive to bees. Some plants have evolved to look like female bees, so males are tricked into trying to mate with them, pollinating them in the process – a process called pseudo-copulation. And recently, scientists even discovered that some plants make their nectar deliberately sweeter if bees are buzzing close by – evening primrose flowers, for instance, can 'sense' when bees are approaching and quickly make their nectar 20 per cent sweeter to try to encourage the insect to land.

Nectar is usually found right at the back of the flower head, so bees have evolved tongues that are really good at reaching this sweet substance and sucking it up. Some bees have short tongues, for shallow flowers, others have long tongues, for deep, tubular-shaped varieties. Some bees are generalists and can drink nectar from a wide variety of plants. Many bees, however, are specialists and have tongues that have evolved to closely match only a certain range of flower: flowers such as honeysuckle or columbine, for example, are too deep for short-tongued bees; equally, long tongues aren't efficient at working shallow flowers. This makes specialist bees vulnerable to changes in the environment, as they can feed from only a few types of flowers. That's why planting just one species of flower doesn't help all kinds of bees.

Some plants make their nectar deliberately sweeter if bees are buzzing close by

We're also slowly discovering just how varied wild bees' diet really is. We think we know what kinds of plants bees prefer but they keep surprising us: one fascinating study carried out by bee ecologist Noah Wilson-Rich looked into the plant DNA found in various samples of honey in Provincetown,

New England. What he discovered was that much of the honey made in the springtime came from privet, summer honey from water lilies, and autumn honey from sumac – none of these three being plants we immediately associate with bees. He also found just how varied different environments were in terms of plant diversity and bee foraging: honey from rural areas had around 150 different plants species in each sample; honey from suburban areas had far fewer, around 100 plants per sample. And most surprising of all, the city honey had a whopping 200 plant species in each sample – in other words, urban

Urban centres were proving to be hugely important for bees and their search for different kinds of flowers

_____

centres were proving to be hugely important for bees and their search for different kinds of flowers. Far from being bad for pollinators, cities may be one of the best places for bees – especially if the suburbs are covered with lawn and rural land is taken up with monoculture farming.

HOW TO HELP BEES

Now that we know what bees are struggling against, we can target our support. Everyone can do something. Whether it's buying local honey or planting your garden full of bee-friendly flowers, there are lots of positive ways to help. The following pages are packed with ways to improve your local environment, shop with bees in mind, get involved with changing policy or teach yourself more about bees. These include:

CONSUMER CHOICES

Buying products and food that promote bee health

HABITAT IMPROVEMENT

Making your environment better for bees

PESTICIDE USE

Limiting the use of any chemicals known to harm bees

RESPONSIBLE BEEKEEPING

Supporting ethical, high-welfare beekeeping

BEE EDUCATION

Learning about and passing on information about bees

GET CAMPAIGNING

Using your voice to improve the long-term future for bees

RESEARCH

Helping science gain a better picture of what's happening
to bee populations

50
Ways
to Help
Save the
Bees

1

Buy Ethical Honey

There's a huge demand for honey. What used to be a sweet treat has become a breakfast staple – the US consumes somewhere around 1.5 pounds of honey per capita every year. To meet the demand, we import the vast majority from countries who produce honey on an industrial scale, such as China and Thailand.

One of the issues with industrial bee farming is that it doesn't seem to do the native bee or the hive bee populations much good.

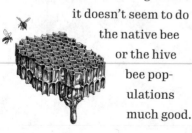

Some of the practices, such as the routine use of antibiotics or killing the bees when the honey is harvested, don't sit comfortably with people who care about animal welfare. Keeping bees in such large, intensive farms has also been linked to problems with hive pests and diseases, which can then transfer to native populations.

Beyond bee health, there are also issues such as poor welfare for bee workers, the impact of food miles, and cheap honey being cut with corn syrup or fructose syrup. According to research, honey is the third most faked food in the world, much of the adulterated product ending up in honey-flavoured foods and products.

The reality is that beekeeping exists on a spectrum – from the intensive and damaging but high yielding at one extreme to conservation beekeeping at the other, where no honey is taken and the bees are left to their own devices (see 41. *Learn About Natural Beekeeping*). The nearer the conservation end of the scale, the better it is for honey bees, but where does that leave our love of honey? If you want to eat honey, there are a few guidelines to help you make ethical choices that benefit both pollinators and people:

- **Buy honey from local beekeepers,** who are more likely to practise small-scale, sustainable beekeeping. Many beekeepers are enthusiasts and treat honey as a by-product, not the sole aim.
- **If you can't buy local, look for certified organic or Fairtrade honey** – it should at least guarantee better environmental and working conditions.
- **Know what you are buying.** 'Pure' and 'Natural' on honey labels mean little in terms of a legal definition,

whereas 'Organic' and 'Fairtrade' have strict criteria. Filtered and pasteurised honey are thought to contain less of the health benefits of raw honey.

- **Approach honey like buying wine.** Provenance is king. Go for single variety honey, from a specific area, rather than cheaper, blended honey from a mix of countries.

2

The Bee-Friendly Food Basket

As a consumer, you have the power to help bees by making conservation-minded decisions every time you shop. It might seem like a small gesture but the collective might of informed customers can persuade lots of different companies to adopt bee-friendly approaches and help enterprises who actively support bees and other pollinators through the products they make, grow or sell.

BUY LOCAL

By buying locally grown food you are often supporting smaller, more biodiverse farms. Intensive, large-scale agriculture often relies on high-yield, single crops; local growers, because they don't have to worry as much about growing for shelf life, supermarket 'perfection' or long-distance transport, can grow a wider range of varieties, including heritage ones. These add to the biodiversity of the countryside. Small-scale, traditional mixed farms also don't tend to farm as intensively – using fewer chemicals, leaving larger wildlife margins and focusing on seasonal crops.

BUY ORGANIC

Organic farming practices can help bees and other pollinators. Organic farms don't use toxic pesticides – this contributes to healthier and more stable populations of bees and butterflies; organic farms also tend to have more floral diversity than conventional farms, thanks to minimal use of herbicides and less intensive practices, which means a larger and more varied group of pollinating insects can thrive. Look for certified organic labels. There are dozens of different schemes, from regional to international – here are just a few:

BUY BEE-FRIENDLY

There are a number of schemes, worldwide, that have been designed to point consumers towards bee-friendly products and foods. In Europe, the certified **Bee Friendly** label is given to companies and farmers who work in harmony with pollinators. In the US, a similar scheme – the Xerces Society's **Bee Better Certified** seal – is used to show that a producer is conservation-minded and incorporates pollinator well-being into their supply chain. Any restaurants showing the **Bee Friendly Food Alliance** logo in their window or on the menu are also committed to protecting bees and banning harmful pesticides. Canada has the **Bee Friendly Farming** logo, which producers can use to show they support agricultural practices that encourage pollinator health.

3

Buy Organic Cotton

———

Cotton farming is a polluting business and ranks among the highest users of pesticides, including those known to be harmful to bees. Buying certified organic cotton – which doesn't use chemicals that damage people or pollinators – means you can wear fabric that's not only kind to humans but also keeps the planet healthy in the process. Look for the Soil Association logo or the Global Organic Textile Standard label on everything from fashion to homeware.

4

Make a Solitary Bee Home

Give solitary bees somewhere to live and they'll reward you by pollinating your flowers and vegetable garden. Not all bee homes are created equal, however. When it comes to making a living space for solitary bees, three things are critical – the bees must be protected from wet weather; the holes must be the right size; and it's important to keep diseases and pests at bay.

The easiest type of solitary bee house to make at home uses lengths of bamboo cane, packed into a container. There are numerous ways you can do this – fill a length of drainpipe, a large plastic bottle with the ends cut off, an old wooden champagne box or drawer, or make a frame for the lengths of bamboo to fit into. If you don't have bamboo cane, you can use other hollow dry stems, paper straws or reeds.

Whichever way you choose to make your solitary bee home, the following conditions should be met for the bees to thrive:

- A bee home needs to be dry. Hang it out of the rain or give the bee home an overhang/sloping roof to deflect rain.

- Holes in the bamboo canes should be between 2mm and 10mm (0.08–0.4 inch) – any bigger and solitary bees won't use them.

- Sharp edges or splinters need to be sanded off – bees won't nest in canes that could injure them.

- One end of the cane needs to be blocked up. Cut the bamboo canes so that one end finishes on a node or seal the ends with wax.

- Replace empty bamboo canes every two years, at the end of summer. This helps prevent any attacks from fungus, parasites and mites.

- Don't replace a 'plugged' bamboo cane unless nothing has emerged for two years (the contents will be dead) or it has a tiny hole in the plug (which is a sign that the bee larvae has been attacked by the *Cacoxenus indagator* fly). In both these cases, the cane should be removed and destroyed.

- Site the bee home in full sun, facing south or south-east, and at least 1 m (3 ft) from the ground. Keep the entrance to the bee home clear of vegetation.

- To give the nesting baby bees an extra chance to survive, move them into a dry shed in October. Put them outside again in March.

5

Make a Mason Bee Home

Mason bees suffer from bad PR. People assume they're called 'mason' bees because they bore holes into bricks and mortar, causing damage, but their name actually comes from their habit of 'bricking up' their nest cells with mud.

The reality is that mason bees, one of the solitary bee families, *do* like small cavities but they don't tend to make them. Female bees are opportunistic, seeking out suitable nest sites – usually hollow plant stems, cavities in dead wood or holes in walls – and

laying their eggs inside, sealing up the chamber with mud they've collected. Walls of period buildings, which are often pointed with soft lime mortar, can be a favourite nesting site because they provide plenty of nail holes, lost mortar joints, cracks and crevices between bricks. Modern cement is often too strong for mason bees.

One of the things that most people don't know about mason bees is just how effective they are at pollinating plants – research has shown that one female mason bee can do as much pollinating as over a hundred honey bees. This is because they will fly in cooler weather, visit more flowers per minute, and are 'clumsier' with their pollen loads (increasing the chances of loose pollen being transferred between plants). They also happen to be one of the friendliest bees around – male mason bees can't sting you and females will only sting if squashed between your fingers.

Mason bees are, therefore, truly the gardener's friend. And while mason bees will happily live in a bamboo bee house (see 4. *Make A Solitary Bee Home*), they will also appreciate a clay bee house or Bee Brick™. You can buy commercially made bee bricks, which can be built into a wall or building or left to stand alone in a garden (see Directory, p. 125). Or you could make your own:

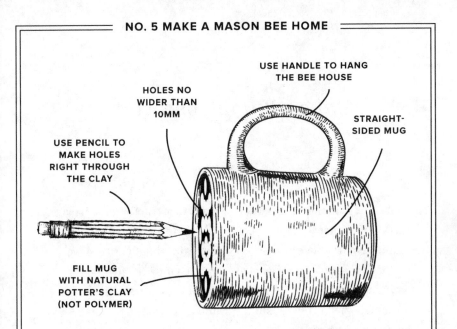

USE HANDLE TO HANG
THE BEE HOUSE

HOLES NO
WIDER THAN
10MM

STRAIGHT-
SIDED MUG

USE PENCIL TO
MAKE HOLES
RIGHT THROUGH
THE CLAY

FILL MUG
WITH NATURAL
POTTER'S CLAY
(NOT POLYMER)

1. Hang or fix your bee brick or mug at least 1 metre (3 feet) off the ground, in a sunny south-facing place.

2. Don't let any plants or other obstructions block the holes and make sure there are plenty of pollinator-friendly plants nearby.

3. It's vital that the mug is hanging horizontally, or slightly tilted forwards, otherwise the holes will fill with rainwater.

4. Clean the holes in your bee home using a pipe cleaner once the cavities are empty (or if you are sure they have failed – see p. 34).

6

Make a Bumblebee Home

—

Different bumblebees nest in different places. Some are happy to nest above ground – in long grass or a pile of leaves – while others prefer underground homes, often reusing abandoned mouse and vole nests, which are full of dry, cosy bedding material. Tree bumblebees will often take over a bird box if it's got an old nest in it.

Getting bumblebees to nest in a commercial bee box is almost impossible, not least because few are designed with the needs of bumblebees in mind. So, what can you do if you want to attract bumblebees to nest in your garden? The first aim should be to leave an area untidy – patches of long grass, piles of leaves and compost heaps make ideal nesting places for many species. Leaving a bird box stuffed with dried moss or an old nest may also attract tree bumblebees. For underground nesting bumblebees, the task is a bit trickier, not least because they're very picky about their sites; the wish list for these bumblebees is somewhere dry, dark, warm and full of snuggly, fine nesting material.

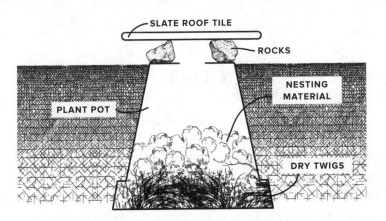

SLATE ROOF TILE

ROCKS

NESTING MATERIAL

PLANT POT

DRY TWIGS

One option is to create an underground cavity with an upturned, buried plant pot. The base of the hole should be lined with criss-crossed twigs, and then fine, natural nesting materials placed on top – dry moss, sheep fleece, upholsterers' cotton or hay (but not straw, which is too coarse). The bee can then climb through the hole in the bottom of the pot. To stop rain coming in and damaging the nest, a roofing slate or similar flat surface can be balanced over the pot hole without blocking it. Don't be disheartened if bumblebees don't take to it straight away – you may find that a mouse nests in it first. This is useful, as next year the old nesting material will make your bumblebee home even more inviting to flying guests (it's thought that bumblebees are keenly attuned to the smell of old rodent nests).

7

Build a Log Pile

—

Carpenter bees make their nests by tunnelling into wood. They're solitary bees, but some make nests alongside their sisters and daughters, creating a small social group. They tend to like dead wood – old tree trunks and timber stacks – so it's easy to create a welcoming habitat for them by building a log pile at the end of the garden. It can be as neat or messy as you like. Choose a sunny spot if possible; carpenter bees seem to favour dry wood rather than damp, rotting timber.

8

Mow Less

Research has shown that people who mow their lawns once a fortnight over summer have more bees than those who mow every week. A study showed that lawns that were trimmed every two weeks had a third more bees than weekly cut grass; the difference is largely thanks to an increase in the number of flowers in longer grass. Interestingly, although gardens that only had their lawns cut every three weeks had more flowers, they didn't have a higher number of bees – researchers think that grass that is too long made it more difficult for the bees to reach the flowers. That said, patches of long grass in spring are essential as nesting sites for solitary bees and bumblebees.

9

Grow Herbs for Bees

Many herbs provide nectar-rich flowers that draw in lots of different kinds of bees. Most flower over summer but some provide food for foraging pollinators from late spring until early autumn. They're also hugely versatile and hard-working plants, with uses ranging from cooking ingredients to medicinal cures, and will suit every outdoor space, from a container to a country garden. Ten of the most bee-friendly include:

BORAGE – a beautiful, blue- or white-flowered herb that you can sow from seed and will bloom for weeks, from late spring right through until autumn. Both the leaves and flowers taste of cucumber, so make the perfect ingredient for salads, cocktails and summer puddings.

CHIVES – an easy-to-grow perennial herb renowned for its onion-tasting leaves and pink-purple flowers through-out summer (you may even get a second flowering if you cut them back after the first flowers have finished). The flowers are also edible and make a pretty garnish.

FENNEL – closely related to the fennel bulb, this large self-seeding perennial also tastes of aniseed and produces clusters of tiny yellow flowers during midsummer. Use the leaves fresh or dry the seeds for a liquorice hit. Also look out for bronze fennel.

HYSSOP – a less well-known herb, closely related to mint. During midsummer, the bees will flock to its spikes of purple-blue flowers on woody stems. Its strong-tasting, slightly bitter leaves have a flavour of sage and mint combined. Use hyssop flowers in salads.

LEMON BALM – another member of the mint family, lemon balm is a bushy perennial with creamy white or pale purple flowers throughout summer. The leaves are delicious, with a lemony zing, and can be added to sweet and savoury dishes, or dried for potpourri.

MARJORAM – a close cousin of oregano, marjoram is a hugely versatile herb whose leaves can be added to pasta sauces, soups and meat dishes, or to flavour oils and vinegars. The flowers – which blossom in summer and continue into early autumn – are also edible.

MINT – a perennial herb so vigorous it's best kept in a pot, mint provides white or pinkish flowers in midsummer that bees find difficult to resist. Use the leaves for herbal infusions, salads, sauces, salsa verde, puddings and summer drinks.

ROSEMARY – a plant that keeps going all year round, this hardy but deliciously fragrant herb has a long flowering season that can start as early as spring. Hugely versatile – it can be grown into a hedge, a shrub or kept as a pot plant, and the leaves used fresh or dried.

SAGE – a pungent herb (also known as culinary sage) that makes a great companion to meat, bean and root vegetable dishes, sage also produces exquisite spikes of light blue, pink or purple flowers throughout summer that can be used in salads or as a garnish.

THYME – perfect in a pot, a border or as a low-growing 'carpet', thyme is a resilient, wonderfully aromatic herb. There are lots of different varieties – some, like 'Jekka', will flower twice, once in late spring and again in summer, making them perfect for pollinators.

10

Plant Trees for Bees

___

We often imagine bees buzzing among the flower beds, but trees are a really valuable source of food for solitary, bumble and honey bees. They're rich, densely packed store cupboards of pollen and nectar, often blossoming earlier and later in the season than flowers; it's estimated that five established trees provide a haul of pollen and nectar equal to an acre of meadow. Trees also provide a place for bees to overwinter and nest, as well as offering shelter for bees who might get caught out by a sudden spell of bad weather. So, if you're planning to replant the garden and have space for a tree or two, consider the following bee-friendly species:

FEB	MAR	APR	MAY
Mimosa	Common hazel	Field maple	Sycamore
Common alder	Cob hazel	Laburnum	Horse chestnut
Rosebud cherry	Cherry plum	Judas tree	Hawthorn
Pussy willow / goat willow	Common plum	Quince	Apple
Common gorse	Blackthorn / sloe	Sweetgum	Snowdrop tree
Viburnum	Forsythia	Crab apple	Holly
	Amelanchier	Wild cherry	Medlar
	Sweet almond	Pear	Rowan / Mountain ash
		Oak	Whitebeam

JUN	JUL	AUG	SEP	OCT
Tulip tree	Sweet chestnut	Indian bean tree	Pagoda tree / honey tree	Loquat tree
Hop tree	Broad leaf lime	Bush brush	Bee-bee tree	Strawberry tree
False acacia	Western gorse / dwarf gorse	Privet	Henry's lime	
Rose acacia		Buddleia		
Common lime		Japanese angelica tree		
Siberian pea tree				

11

Grow Blooms for Bees

———

A garden should have a rich variety of flowering plants, covering as much of the growing season as possible. Late summer is often a difficult time for bees, for example, as food can be in short supply. Look at flowers through the eyes of a bee to see whether they offer obvious sources of nectar and pollen – long-tongued bumblebees like deep, tubular flowers such as foxgloves and lavender, while short-tongued honey bees prefer shallow, open-centred blooms such as borage and sedums. A mix of different

flowers will provide food for lots of different kinds of bees and butterflies. Below is just a small selection of bees' favourite plants but look for labels such as 'plants for pollinators' or 'bee friendly':

NO. 11 GROW BLOOMS FOR BEES

BULBS*	ANNUALS / BIENNIALS	PERENNIALS	SHRUBS	CLIMBERS
Crocus	Cosmos	Salvias	Lavender	Honeysuckle
Bluebells	Viper's bugloss	Catmint	Escallonia	Clematis
Fritillaries	Cornflowers	Sedums	Fuchsia	Ivy
Aconites	Candytuft	Sea holly	Broom	Hops
Grape hya-	Nigella	Verbena	Roses	Wisteria
cinths	Foxgloves	Persicaria	(single-	Passion
Hyacinths	Zinnias	Penstemon	flower)	flower
Leucojum	Sunflowers	Hellebores	Dog rose	Sweet pea
Alliums	Poppies	Agastache	Ceanothus	Jasmine
Snowdrops	Sneezeweed	Bird's-foot	Spring and	Buddleia
	Hollyhocks	trefoil	winter	Pyracantha
	Evening	Dahlias	heather	Virginia
	primrose	(single-	Bee bush	creeper
	Forget-me-nots	flower)	(abelia)	Climbing
		Lambs' ears	Mahonia	hydrangea
		Scabious	Teucrium	
		Thrift	Hebe	
		Veronica	Manuka	
		Meadowsweet	Lacecap	
		Aquilegia	hydrangea	
		Verbascum		
		Astrantia		
		Chrysan-		
		themum		
		Yarrow		

*See 23. *Buy Neonicotinoid-free Bulbs.*

12

Swap a Fence for a Hedge

Hedgerows are another valuable source of nectar and pollen for bees and other pollinators. If you need to replace a garden boundary or put in a new one, plant a hedge. Fences offer nothing in terms of cover, food or nesting places for bugs (or any other wildlife), while a hedge can soon become a refuge for bees, birds and garden-friendly mammals such as hedgehogs. Go for a species of hedge that's rich in blossom – such as hawthorn or rosemary – or even better, plant a mixed hedge that will give successive flowers throughout the year.

13

Bye-Bye Bedding Plants

Nothing says summer more than a garden full of blousy flowers, the air heavy with the buzz of foraging bees. And yet, not all flowers are equal when it comes to pollinating insects. Such is our desire to produce strange, ornamental hybrids that many flowers are useless for bees. Most bedding plants, for instance, provide very little nutrition for bees, while some common varieties of perennials, such as dahlias, have been interbred to produce pom-pom heads, making it tricky for insects to reach the pollen and nectar. In general, steer clear of most bedding plants – things like Busy Lizzies, some types of French marigold, pansies and begonias – doubleflower varieties, and other highly hybridised plants that offer little in terms of food for bees.

14

Plant Fruit & Vegetables for Bees

———

Certain food-producing plants provide a hearty supply of pollen and/or nectar, even in a small-sized garden or allotment. We also rely on bees to pollinate a vast shopping list of our favourite fruits and vegetables, from sour cherries to blueberries, apples to avocados. Even plants that don't rely on insects for their pollination seem to benefit from a bee visit; strawberries, for example, don't need bees for pollination (they're self-fertile and can pollinate themselves) but studies have shown that they produce more fruit, bigger, brighter berries and lower numbers of deformed berries when they're pollinated by bees. Some food crops also don't need bees to produce fruit but may need them to make seeds.

You may find that only certain types of bees visit certain plants, while others will be universally popular. Planting a wide variety of fruit and vegetables, especially those that don't flower at the same time, should provide a wide window of

FRUIT BUSHES	FRUIT TREES	OTHER FRUITS & VEGETABLES
Raspberry	Apple	Green bean
Blackberry	Crab apple	Broad bean
Bilberry	Pear	Pea
Blueberry	Gage	Tomato
Redcurrant	Damson	Pepper
Blackcurrant	Plum	Chilli
Whitecurrant	Medlar	Aubergine
Gooseberry	Quince	Squash
Loganberry	Sweet cherry	Pumpkin
Boysenberry	Sour cherry	Melon
Dewberry	Sweet almond	Cucumber
Wineberry	Peach	Courgette
Tummelberry	Nectarine	Strawberry
Tayberry	Orange	Wild strawberry
	Lemon	
	Kiwi	

opportunity for bees, butterflies and other beneficial bugs. Some plants – such as kale or broccoli – may not seem like obvious food for bees, but if allowed to go to seed will also produce masses of bee-attracting flowers.

15

Make a Wildflower Area

Wildflower meadows were once a nectar- and pollen-rich source of food for bees. But for decades, wildflower meadows have been in decline, a loss of habitat that has had a devastating impact not only on pollinating insects but also on small mammals and wild birds. Gardeners, councils and landowners can help, however, by creating wildflower areas – however big or small. They're not only beneficial to bees but they also happen to be beautiful to look at and low maintenance once they're established.

Getting started is the hardest bit. A good chunk of work needs to go into preparing the site and cutting the meadow at the right time. But once the meadow or wildflower patch is established, you'll soon find it's a mecca for wildlife. Different regions worldwide will have optimum times, so check with your wildflower seed supplier.

PREPARE – the first thing to do is clear the ground you plan to sow. Choose somewhere open and sunny. Certain grasses and weeds will compete with wildflowers, making it difficult for them to get established, so you need to remove them. People usually do this one of three ways – either physically, by digging out the contents of a patch; using a turf cutter to remove the top layer; or spraying it off using a *glyphosate* weed-killer (*glyphosate* use is a thorny issue, however, and the subject of conflicting assessments about its effect on bees and human health). You then need to rotavate the area and rake to a fine, crumbly tilth.

SOW – choose a mix that suits your soil type but, crucially, contains an annual plant called yellow rattle. Yellow rattle interferes with the roots of aggressive

grasses, weakening them to allow wildflowers and more suitable grasses to thrive. Sow your seeds according to the supplier's recommendations (usually about 5g of seed per square metre/¼ oz per 1½ square yards). Mix the seed with kiln dried paving sand (about 6 parts sand to 1 part seed) – this helps dilute the seed to make sowing easier and helps you see where you've sown. Roller or trample the seeds to compress them into the soil. You can also get wild seed turf, which is ready to lay.

CUT – cut the wildflower area in August or September with the mower on its highest setting or using a scythe or strimmer (always check for hedgehogs and other daytime nesting animals first). Leave the cuttings for a week, so the seeds can fall off, and then rake up and compost. Cut again in early spring if it needs it.

MAINTAIN – you may, over the years, find that certain species start to dominate. You can vary the time you cut the wildflowers, sow extra seeds, do spot weeding or plant out wildflower 'plug' seedlings to keep the balance in check.

16

Leave the Compost Heap Alone

—

Gardeners divide into two camps when it comes to compost heaps – the turners and the non-turners. When you make compost, oxygen is the vital ingredient that helps organic material decompose. The idea is that turning the compost with a garden fork adds more air and speeds up the rotting process. The problem with turning, however, is that lots of bugs, including bees and small mammals, also like to live and nest in compost

heaps, especially over spring and summer. If you want to be kinder to bees, try no-turn composting. The key is balancing the amount of nitrogen-rich material you put in (such as grass cuttings or vegetable scraps) with brown, 'fluffier' materials that provide pockets of air (dry leaves, straw, shredded paper). The process of decomposition takes a little longer than turned compost, but in time the microbes and other bugs in the material will slowly help the compost break down, without disturbing the bees, beetles, hedgehogs and other creatures that might have decided to make your compost heap their home. And if you do want to empty your compost heap, leaving it until autumn will ensure that many of its inhabitants have already gone their merry ways.

17

Leave the Ivy

———

Autumn is the time many gardeners put their plots 'to bed', cutting back, pruning and digging up annuals in time for winter. But one plant should be left well alone: ivy is one of the few flowering plants left for bees and late butterflies in autumn, and the berries that appear in early winter are a vital source of food for wild birds. Leave pruning the ivy until after the last berries have been gobbled up.

18

Make a Wild Pond

———

Wild ponds, however small, can support a huge range of creatures – from frogs and toads to dragonflies and bees. We don't tend to make a link between loss of natural ponds and insects, but the drainage and disappearance of wild wetlands, streams and other water features has had a direct impact on the decline of bees, dragonflies and other insects, as well as birds, bats and other small mammals. Bees, in particular, use ponds in four ways: if it's shallow enough, or has floating plants, a pond is an essential source of drinking water for bees; flowering pond and bog plants, such as lilies, water forget-me-not and water mint, provide much-needed food for foraging bees; the sandy banks that surround ponds and rivers are often used as bee burrows; and reeds, which grow in wet ground and alongside the edges of ponds, also provide vital nesting sites. Wild About Gardens has a fantastic introduction to making a wild pond, 'Big or small, ponds for all', which is free to download (see Directory, p. 125).

19

Love the Weeds

———

Don't be too hasty to create an immaculate garden – bees are particularly fond of common weeds such as dandelions, clover, buttercups, celandines, bramble, bird's-foot trefoil, cow parsley, white dead nettle, milkweed and poppies.

20

Garden for Bumblebees

———

Bumblebees have suffered huge declines over recent years. In the US, the formerly common rusty patched bumblebee is endangered, and you're 50 per cent less likely to see bumblebees in North America than you were in the 1970s. And yet, ironically, the bumblebee is one of the nation's most loved insects, often viewed as the fatter, fluffier, gentler cousin of the honey bee.

Our gardens have become a valuable refuge for bumblebees, with city plots often providing more attractive habitats for bees than intensively farmed areas. Recent research in Germany, for example, found that bumblebees are more successful at pollinating urban areas than agricultural land, with city parks, green spaces and urban gardens

having a higher flower diversity and more potential nesting areas.

It's also a two-way relationship – a fascinating study looking at field mustard showed that when pollinated by bumblebees, as opposed to other insects, the flowers evolved to be taller, bloom earlier and have double the fragrance over the space of just a few years. Scientists concluded that the bees preferred the taller, highscented plants and so pollinated those instead of the shorter varieties with less fragrance. Over just a few generations, the bigger, more perfumed plants thrived.

So, whether you have a window box or access to an allotment, a generous back garden or a shared outside space, there are some simple ways to encourage bumblebees to visit:

- Most bumblebees prefer **perennial** flowers that come up year after year. Traditional 'cottage garden' plants and flowering herbs are ideal (see 11. *Grow Blooms for Bees*).

- Plants are more useful to bumblebees if planted in **large, same-variety groups** or drifts. Bumblebees tend to stick to one type of flower when they're hunting for food and can waste too much energy flitting between disparate flowers.

- Bumblebees need a constant food supply between spring and autumn – plan for plants that **flower in succession**, rather than all at once.

- Bumblebees have evolved to have different tongue lengths to match the flowers they feed on. This reduces competition for the same flowers between species of bumblebees. Bumblebees with long tongues, for example, can make use of long tubular flowers, while shorter-tongued species will collect nectar from shallower flowers. Providing a **mix of flower shapes** – from the tubular to bell- or bowl-shaped – will allow a greater variety of bumblebees to feed.

- Leave a **wild, informal corner** of the garden for bumblebees to nest. Different species like different habitats – some will nest under sheds or in compost heaps, others like tussocky grass, hedgerows or soil banks.

21

Put up Extra Bird Boxes

Tree bees are well known for squatting in abandoned bird boxes. As more and more wildlife competes for limited resources around towns and cities, there have been incidents of bees and wild birds, such as blue tits, competing for somewhere to nest. Help both the birds and the bees by putting up multiple bird boxes in different locations around your garden. That way, there should be enough nesting sites to go around.

22

Build a Bee Drinker

We're still learning lots about how honey bees use water. One of the things we do know, however, is how important water is in helping to cool the hive. When the weather fluctuates, the temperature inside the hive needs to be consistent. On hot sunny days, certain worker bees are tasked with collecting water. These 'water carriers' fly out of the hive, fill their bellies with water and come home. They then regurgitate the water, and other worker bees fan the water to help it evaporate. Like a natural air-conditioning system, the evaporating water brings down the temperature of the hive, keeping the eggs and developing brood from overheating. We also know that honey bees use water to dilute the food that is given to the queen and larvae in the hive. A typical wild hive is estimated to need around 25 litres (5½ imperial gallons) of water a year.

One of the interesting things is that – given the choice – bees seem to prefer slightly salty water. The nutrients in salty water might be essential for the developing brood of honey bees but researchers have also seen solitary bees (that is, those who don't live in a hive) occasionally drinking water. Quite why this is, we don't know. One thought is that lots of different types of bees might also need, from time to time, to supplement their diet of nectar with salts from water.

In the wild, bees use many different sources of water – from muddy puddles to the margins of shallow ponds, animal urine to sea water. During hot, dry summers, bees can struggle to find adequate sources of water and end up risking a drink from a swimming pool or drinking agricultural run-off, which can often contain harmful levels of pesticides. But we can help.

Creating a 'bee drinker' – whether it's in your garden or on a window ledge – will help bees and other pollinators find a useful source of water.

- It's easy – they just need a saucer or shallow dish of tap water, filled with marbles or pebbles so that any insects who land can drink without drowning.

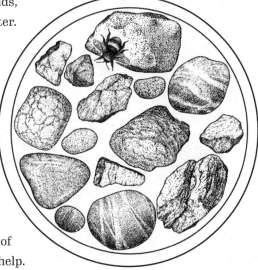

- Bees need to be able to get close to a source of water without risk of falling in, preferring to drink from wet surfaces rather than deep pools of water.
- If you haven't got a shallow dish, a deeper vessel will do but you just need to make sure there are plenty of floating 'bee rafts' for them to land on, such as wine corks or lollipop sticks.
- Just keep topping up as the water level drops.
- If you have space, create a wild pond that'll support lots of different wildlife including bees (see 18. *Make a Wild Pond*).

23

Buy Neonicotinoid-free Bulbs

———

One of the ironies of gardening for bees is that some of the very plants we choose to help bees might be harming them. There's been some concern that many conventionally grown bulbs are sprayed with neonicotinoids, which can then stay in the flower for weeks (if not months) afterwards, potentially affecting any flying insects who visit them. There's a growing number of companies who provide zero-pesticide bulbs – such as the Organic Gardening Catalogue, Crocus or Natural Bulbs – but garden centres are also beginning to stock sustainable bulbs (see Directory, p. 125).

24

Sign Up for a Free Packet of Seeds

———

There have been a number of recent initiatives to distribute bee-friendly seeds and wildflower mixes. They differ from year to year but a quick internet search should throw up a handful of organisations who are handing out free seeds – either on an individual basis or to schools and other charitable organisations. One recent UK campaign, by the Royal Botanic Gardens, Kew, handed out 100,000 free packets of seeds, encouraging people to turn their gardens, window boxes and allotments into wildflower paradises. A similar project in Canada,

'Bees Matter', provided over 250,000 seed packets, which, if successfully planted, will create over 1,250,000 square feet of pollinator-friendly gardens.

Companies are also getting in on the act – Just Bee drinks, for example, give away free wildflower seeds on their website, Innocent smoothies have a free growing kit for schools, and seed merchant Grow Seed runs a 'seeds for schools' programme, handing out free seeds for school garden clubs or class activities.

Look out for environmental charities and national

organisations too – Friends of the Earth, for example, send out free Bee Saver Kits (which include wildflower seeds) with every donation. In the US, the University of Rhode Island Cooperative Extension offers free seed packets to schools and community and youth groups, while the Washington State Noxious Weed Control Board have free Bee-U-Tify seed packets filled with native species. The UK's Hardy Plant Society makes seeds available, free of charge, to charities and public bodies involved in gardening, including schools, community wildlife gardens and hospices, and the Woodland Trust gives away free trees and hedging plants to schools – many of which will be pollinator-friendly, such as crab apple and wild cherry.

While many of these schemes may only be temporary, other similar ones will continue to take their place. So, if you're keen to get your hands on some free pollinator-friendly seeds and don't know where to start, try the following places:

- Environmental charities
- Gardening magazines
- Horticultural clubs
- Local authority schemes
- Plant nurseries
- Seed merchants
- Universities/Plant science departments
- Conservation bodies
- Food/beverage companies
- Cosmetic manufacturers
- Online seed exchange forums such as GardenWeb or The Seed Swap

25

Ditch the Pesticides

———

As the pesticide debate rages on, many gardeners and bee lovers are taking matters into their own hands. By taking a broader approach to gardening – and making changes that reduce the need for pesticide use in the first place – many people are finding they can grow and garden without the need for any insect-harming chemicals at all.

COMPANION PLANTING – Create plant relationships that mutually benefit each other, protect crops from pests and improve pollination. Onions, leeks and chives, for example, are thought to discourage carrot fly and aphids. Nasturtiums are regularly planted with brassicas to entice caterpillars away, while mint is traditionally used to deter flea beetles, carrot fly and aphids.

CROP ROTATION – By moving your vegetable crop around a plot, and planting according to a rotational plan, you not only improve soil fertility and weed control but, crucially, you can reduce the build-up of spores, eggs and pests in the soil.

SOIL IMPROVEMENT – Healthy soil produces healthy plants. The easiest way to maintain soil health is to apply a lovely thick layer of compost or mushroom mulch every winter and let the earthworms pull it into the soil. Taking a no-dig approach also seems to create healthier soil (you create beds that are accessible from paths, don't compact the soil by walking on it, and keep adding organic matter to the top).

NATIVE GARDENING – Rather than setting yourself, and nature, an uphill task, choose plants that are suited to your soil, your site and your local climate. Plants that struggle to grow will also struggle to fight off pests and diseases.

USE NATURAL DETERRENTS AND BARRIERS – Look for natural insect sprays – they often contain plant extracts or oils that are bee-friendly but effective on specific garden pests. Biological controls such as nematodes have proved hugely effective on some of the most damaging pests such as vine weevils, white fly and aphids. Practical measures, such as effective netting, natural slug traps and cloches, can also help. Encouraging in other wildlife, such as hedgehogs and wild birds, can also help keep garden pests at bay without resorting to chemicals.

26

Don't Water in Full Sun

Gardeners already know the traditional wisdom about watering plants either early in the morning or early in the evening, to avoid the evaporating effects of the sun. But did you know that it also helps bees if you don't switch on the hosepipe during the day? Bees tend to fly during the warmest hours of the day – usually after breakfast when the air temperature has risen above 13°C (55°F) or before the evening air starts to cool down. And while bees can fly in a light drizzle, getting caught out by a sudden sprinkler or the heavy drops of a hosepipe spray can be lethal. If you need to water your garden, try early morning or early evening, when pollinators have finished for the day. Or, even better, use a watering can or irrigation system that can apply water directly to the soil rather than the foliage.

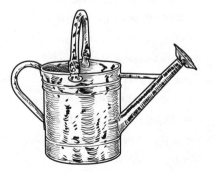

27

Be a Bee-friendly Farmer

___

If you are involved with agriculture, either for business or as a pastime, there are some recognised ways you can help bees and other pollinating insects. Not only will it give bees a boost but research has shown that increasing the number of pollinators on crops can contribute to higher, better- quality yields. The habitats that support bees also support other insects, birds and mammals, many of which are natural predators of crop pests.

There are a number of initiatives, such as Bee Better Certification in the US, that are focused on helping farmers move towards more bee-friendly practices, regardless of the size. In England, the government's Countryside Stewardship scheme provides financial incentives to farmers who implement measures such as planting flower-rich margins. Other measures include:

PROVIDING BEE HABITAT – Asking farmers and smallholders to set aside at least 5 per cent of their land for bee habitat, will help ensure there are abundant sources of nectar and pollen right through the growing season. These can be a mixture of permanent changes, such as planting hedgerows, or seasonal flowering cover crops such as red clover, hairy vetch and buckwheat.

SPACE FOR NEST SITES – Solitary bees need somewhere to live. Sadly, many intensively farmed landscapes don't offer many opportunities for nest building. Bees like untilled ground, grassy thickets, dead wood, leaf litter, small cavities, abandoned birds' nests, plant stems – all the 'untidy' areas. Providing a few wild corners and untamed field borders, with undisturbed ground, hedgerows and banks of soil, will give different kinds of bees (and other wildlife) the chance to thrive.

BUFFER ZONES FOR BEES – Farmers can also help by reducing the use of insecticides and herbicides, which kill either pollinators or the plants they need to survive. Using less toxic alternatives, or employing strategies such as unsprayed buffer zones, avoiding drift, evening spraying and targeted pesticide use, help minimise the exposure of bees to pesticides.

Both the National Farmers' Union and Xerces Society have excellent guides to helping pollinators on your farm (see Directory, p. 125).

28

Leave Some Bare Ground

—

Lots of species of native bee like to nest underground. Most prefer well-drained, crumbly or sandy soils, which make tunnel building easier than compact or waterlogged ground. If you can, leave a patch of your garden bare, preferably on a slope, and ideally south-facing in a warm, sheltered spot. If you've already got a sandy bank, or pile of loose soil, you could make a few holes in it with a pencil and see if it attracts any visitors.

29

Create a Community Bee Garden

———

Public gardens are powerful community spaces. They're important for so many reasons: they provide havens of green space in urban areas, give access to people who may not have their own outdoor space, allow people to come together for a common cause, and give individuals and groups the opportunity to heal, recuperate and learn in a natural setting. A community bee-friendly garden could be sited in any number of places – a churchyard, school ground, hospital garden, park, communal area, university, nursery, care home, commercial premises – anywhere that people can congregate.

Most of the hard work isn't the physical task of digging and planting up a green space, it's issues such as governance, funding, managing volunteers and having a long-term strategy, but there are plenty of organisations willing to help. Groups such as Social Farms and Gardens in the UK or the American Community Gardening

Association can offer advice on how to start a community garden in your neighbourhood, covering areas such as forming a planning committee, securing sponsorship and choosing a suitable site.

While there's no one right way to create a community garden, there are simple steps that you can follow to make a constructive start:

- **IDENTIFY A SPACE** – Find out who owns it and make initial contact. The local council or Land Registry are both good places to start. Bear in mind you'll need a long lease – it'll take the garden at least two years to flourish. Have a persuasive, positive case for the project already worked out – list the potential benefits of the garden.

- **ORGANISE A MEETING** – Ask anyone who might benefit from the garden, not just potential volunteers. Include local businesses, residents, tenants, schools etc. This is an ideas-gathering meeting and a test of local interest; you need to ensure the community is behind you.

- **GET A CORE TEAM TOGETHER** – You need a small committee of dedicated people who have time to commit to the project. Divide up responsibilities based on experience of fundraising, governance, horticulture, health and safety, PR.

- **WORK OUT WHAT YOU NEED**
  – Get a clear idea of a design
  and use it as a basis for
  your costings. If you can get
  professional advice here,
  even better. You also need to
  factor in other key elements
  for a public space, not least
  public liability insurance,
  ongoing maintenance costs
  and risk assessments.

- **FUNDRAISE** – Approach
  sponsors, local businesses,
  crowdfund, get people to
  'adopt' a patch of the garden, or ask for donations via
  social media and targeted
  events. Set up a fundraising page online, such as
  JustGiving, tell the local
  media about your garden,
  and keep people informed of
  your progress.

30

Use Peat-free Compost

———

Peat bogs are a vital wild habitat for a vast range of flora and fauna, including native bees. When peat is extracted to create compost, the bog

is drained and stripped off, destroying the natural environment and the many rare and valuable species that live in it. Peat is also very slow to regenerate – less than 2mm (0.08 inch) a year – while harvesting strips off around 20cm (8 inches) a year. Peat bogs also store huge amounts of carbon dioxide, which are then released back into the atmosphere when disturbed, contributing to climate change. Peat-free compost, which is widely available, is a bee-friendly alternative.

31

Green Up Your Shed

Garden buildings are hugely popular but they have one big drawback – they take up space that could otherwise be occupied by pollinator-friendly plants.

While this might not be an issue in a generous garden, urban spaces are often squeezed for green space. One option is to green up your garden shed by installing a simple living roof.

Not only are green roofs brilliant at attracting insects such as bees and butterflies, they can also benefit your outdoor living space in other ways. Adding more plants will help improve air quality, extend the roof life of your shed, reduce rainwater run-off, and even absorb sunlight, keeping the interior of your garden retreat nice and cool in summer.

Creating a green roof is a book in itself but there are some simple principles behind greening up a shed roof:

1. Plants for a green shed roof need to be pollinator-friendly but also drought tolerant, low maintenance and relatively low-growing. Sedums are a fantastic choice – not least because bees absolutely love them. Other tried-and-tested green roof plants for bees include fescue, thyme, fleabane, dwarf marjoram, thrift, bird's-foot trefoil and saxifrage. Many green roof suppliers now sell plants in a ready-to-lay roll, just like turf, which can be cut to size.

2. Green roofs usually have a 5–10 cm (2–4 inch) layer of lightweight growing medium, a combination of top soil, compost and perlite or grit to help with drainage.

3. Flat roofs or gentle slopes (less than 20°) are easier to convert as there are issues with water and soil retention on steeply sloping sides (although there are green roof systems for steeply pitched roofs). An integrated drainage layer is essential, so the plants don't become waterlogged.

4. You also need a substantial waterproof membrane to stop both moisture and roots penetrating the shed roof. Traditional shed roof asphalt isn't up to the job – you'll need heavy duty rubber or PVC.

5. The shed roof has to be strong enough to take the

extra load – around 60kg per square metre/125lb per square yard (roughly the same as someone standing on the roof). Your shed may need extra bracing in the form of additional roof trusses, joists or other timber supports, and it'll need some form of edging around the sides of the roof. If in doubt, get professional advice.

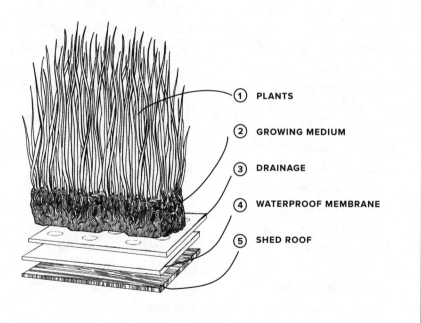

1. PLANTS
2. GROWING MEDIUM
3. DRAINAGE
4. WATERPROOF MEMBRANE
5. SHED ROOF

32

Build a Window Box for Bees

Even if you don't have an outside space, you can still help bees by planting a window box full of pollen- and nectar-rich flowers. As we've already learned, city environments can be a rich and diverse source of food for bees.

Single-species window boxes can look really striking – few things make an impact more than a container full of just lavender, salvias or lupins. Many of the flowers listed earlier in the book (see 11. *Grow Blooms for Bees*) will work brilliantly in containers or window boxes, either planted en masse or as part of an arrangement. Herbs are also a natural for window boxes and will soon be colonised by pollinating insects – try thyme, prostrate rosemary, chives, mint, marjoram (see 9. *Grow Herbs for Bees*).

If you want a window box that will attract a range of bees, or that includes more than one plant species, there are some easy rules to follow that can help you create something that's both beautiful and useful for pollinators:

· **Stick to three plants**
  – go for colours that sit
  next to each other on the

colour wheel (i.e. pinks,
purples, blues) or comple-
mentary opposite colours
(i.e. yellows and purples)
if you want something
eye-catching.

- Just as when you're creating
a flower bouquet, **choose
plants that have differ-
ent forms**. Mix together
something that creates
height or 'spikes of interest' (such as lupins, alliums, poppies or echinops),
something that gives the
window box a solid body
of colour (such as salvias,
lavender, catmint, Mexican
fleabane, heathers), and
something that has glorious,
softening foliage but is still
useful for bees (such as sage,
heuchera, geranium, ivy).

- **Work out what flowers
simultaneously** – you need
everything to look good at

the same time. For example,
a summer window box could
include sage, salvia and
alliums, while an autumn
container would suit bee-
friendly nerines, ivy and
sedum.

- When you're growing
plants in such a confined
space, with the roots
tightly packed together,
**you need a hard-working
compost** that's full of

nutrients and won't dry out too quickly. Go for a good-quality compost and, once you've planted up, dress the surface with a layer of fine grit to keep the moisture trapped in (see 30. *Use Peat-free Compost*).

- Unless you've chosen drought-tolerant plants, you'll need to **water the window box regularly** – every day in summer.

33

Follow #SaveTheBees

—

Social media has been instrumental in spreading the word about bee decline and what can be done to help. Use the hashtag #SaveTheBees on Twitter and Instagram to find out about current campaigns, gardening for bees, scientific research, projects to help pollinators and bee champions across the world.

34

Campaign for Bees

———

There are dozens of motivated, well-informed conservation groups who need your support and help. Whether you simply join and donate every month or get involved at a grass-roots level, campaigning for bees and other pollinating insects *does* make a difference. Many of the larger environmental charities – such as Friends of the Earth, WWF or the RSPB – can effect change at a government level, for instance, by consulting on pesticide policy or setting up pollinator guidelines that local councils can follow.

Large charitable organisations can also fund ground-breaking scientific research into bee populations, set up national accreditation schemes and organise summits, where information and international expertise can be shared.

There are also specialised campaign groups who focus solely on pollinators or certain types of bees. In the US, the Pollinator Friendly Alliance, for example, relies on a dedicated volunteer network to do everything, from habitat installation to advocacy, organising community events to organisational support. Both money and time are two welcome resources, not only for practical conservation work but also for raising awareness.

So, if you want to campaign for bees, there are a number of ways you can help:

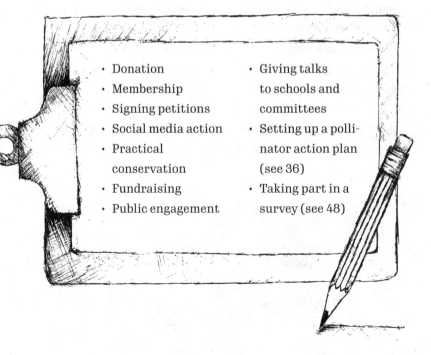

- Donation
- Membership
- Signing petitions
- Social media action
- Practical conservation
- Fundraising
- Public engagement

- Giving talks to schools and committees
- Setting up a pollinator action plan (see 36)
- Taking part in a survey (see 48)

35

Leave a Legacy

———

Anyone can leave money to a bee charity in their will. This is called a legacy. Whether it's £5 or £5,000, it's a fantastic way to do something good with your estate and help safeguard the future of bees. You'll need to add it to your will. There are two simple ways to do this – either write a new will, which will overwrite the old one, or add something called a codicil, which is a document used to make changes to an existing will. You can always talk to your lawyer and discuss your options about leaving a gift to a charity in your will.

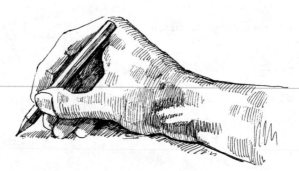

36

Set up a Pollinator Action Plan

One of the most direct ways you can help bees is to get your council to develop its own 'pollinator action plan'. As a member of a democratic community, you have the right to talk to your council about their approach to bees and ways they could help pollinating insects in your local area.

Local councils are vital when it comes to helping bees. They are responsible for huge areas of land, verges, school gardens, parks and other green spaces, all of which could be made more bee-friendly.

They also have significant power when it comes to planning, housing development control and agricultural land management. Perhaps most importantly, local councils can provide leadership and inspiration when it comes to getting the local community involved.

So, how do you get your local council to set up a pollinator action plan? The first thing to do is to **find out who to speak to on the council** – it might be the Countryside Officer, Conservation Officer, Biodiversity Officer or someone with a similar job title. **Work out what you want to achieve**. Friends of the Earth have an excellent guide on how to develop a pollinator plan and examples of success stories, many of which can save councils money in the long run (see Directory, p. 125). Ideas, many of which have already been implemented by forward-thinking councils, include:

- Looking at ways parks can be managed to benefit bees and other pollinators – such as reducing the frequency of grass mowing (see 8. *Mow Less*) or planting new hedges using native flowering species such as hawthorn, goat willow, crab apple or blackthorn (see 12. *Swap a Fence for a Hedge*).

- Creating new wildflower areas in public spaces or reducing the frequency of mowing on road verges to allow wildflowers to grow.

- Providing educational opportunities where children can learn about pollinators and their habitats, including school gardens.

- Developing pollinator feeding stations and nesting sites in built-up areas.

- Limiting the use of bedding plants, which look colourful but offer little for pollinating bugs. Encouraging the planting of trees, bulbs, wildflowers, perennials and flowering shrubs instead.
- Protecting green spaces and allotments from housing development.
- Reducing the council's use of harmful pesticides, including neonicotinoids.
- Raising public awareness through community events, business sponsorship, gardening awards and pop-up stalls.

37

Go on a Beekeeping Course

——

Perhaps the best way to learn about bees is to go on a beekeeping course. The end goal doesn't have to be having your own hive – you might simply want to learn more about bee behaviour, gardening for bees and what you can do to help pollinating insects. It's also a great way to meet fellow bee enthusiasts – the beekeeping community is a warm and generous one, and you're certain to find people more than happy to share their experiences, time and even equipment should you want to take it further.

Beekeeping has also changed in the past few years – it's attracting a wide range of people, young and old, with many people expressing an interest in keeping urban bees, setting up a bee collective, crowdfunding a hive or learning about conservation beekeeping (see 41. *Learn About Natural Beekeeping*), as well as more traditional forms of the craft.

The best place to start is an introductory or taster course – your local beekeeping association or 'chapter' will have the details of training opportunities nearest you. You can also find them via national associations such as the American Beekeeping Federation, who have a list of local clubs and courses online. There are also plenty of smallholdings, city farms and rural enterprises that offer one-day courses, which are ideal if you just want to dip your toe in and see how you feel when you're actually faced with the reality of a living colony.

A typical 'beekeeping for beginners' course will hopefully give you a rounded introduction not only to beekeeping but also to bee anatomy, hive structure, colony behaviour and pests. There should also be opportunities to get out into the field and have a go at some of the practical basics such as making up frames, lighting smokers and honey extraction, depending on the length of the course. If you find you do want to pursue beekeeping, many of the local associations offer a 'try a hive' scheme, where you can hire a hive and basic tools for one full season. At the end of the trial, you can either return the kit or buy it from the association.

38

Loan Your Land

If you don't want to keep bees yourself but would like to help beekeepers, why not offer your garden or land as a space for hives? You can do this in a number of ways – your local beekeeping chapter (which you can find through the national association) will often pair landowners and beekeepers together, or you might be able to arrange something through an online beekeeping or smallholding/farming forum. You could also advertise your space through a community noticeboard or local organization newsletter.

Most 'contracts' between

beekeeper and landowner are informal, while rent is typically a jar of honey per hive per year. Not all land is suitable for beehives – keepers will usually be looking for somewhere easily accessible by vehicle, sheltered, sunny and with plenty of local forage throughout the season. They'll also want to check the situation with neighbouring land and any potential contact with agricultural sprays.

39

Report a Bee Kill

—

Whether you are a concerned beekeeper or a member of the public, if you suspect pesticides have been responsible for killing the contents of a

hive or for the sudden death of over 200 bees, you need to report it to the relevant bodies. This isn't just so that people who are using illegal pesticides are caught, it also gives the government a better idea of how legal pesticides might be affecting bees. Pesticides are often the cause of sudden die-offs of honey bees, usually when they've been directly sprayed or been contaminated by spray drift. If bee kills aren't reported, the government agencies responsible for regulating pesticides will assume that a particular pesticide is safe. The information that can be gathered from bee kills also helps scientists pinpoint more accurately which pesticides or active ingredients are causing harm.

In the US, bee kills should be reported to the Environmental Protection Agency (beekill@epa.gov).

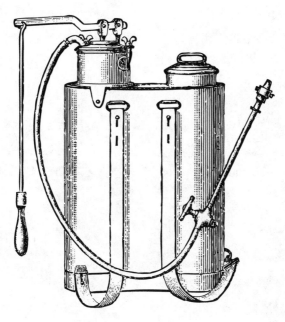

40

Never Feed Bees Honey

———

Never leave supermarket honey out for bees.

Honey from unknown sources can carry diseases, such as foul brood, which although not harmful to humans can pass from hive to hive, or from hive to wild bee populations.

41

Learn About Natural Beekeeping

——

While habitat loss, chemicals and disease are well-established arguments in the debate about bee decline, a growing number of people are starting to wonder whether the way we keep bees, especially on a large commercial scale, might be contributing to their decline. Some of the routine practices involved with industrial honey farming – such as artificial feeding regimes, use of antibiotics or preventing colonies from swarming – may be 'stressing' bees and interfering with their natural resistance to certain diseases and pests.

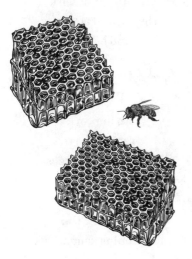

A new approach is gaining momentum – called 'apicentric' or natural beekeeping. It focuses on a type of beekeeping that aims to keep bees in hives more suited to their natural behaviour and needs, rather than the convenience of the beekeeper. Practices such as allowing the bees to swarm naturally, not feeding bees with sugar, disturbing the bees as infrequently as possible, and allowing the bees to build their own combs are commonplace, along with using hives that are designed to mimic the sites that wild honey bees would choose. Some of these hives allow you to harvest honey – such as the Warre or top bar. Others, such as tree hives or sun hives (which look a bit like old-fashioned skeps), are built with bee conservation in mind, not honey harvesting. A key area of focus for all types of natural beekeeping, however, is to try to work with the natural rhythms and behaviour of wild honey bee colonies in an attempt to improve their resistance to disease and boost numbers.

Opinion is mixed among the beekeeping community

– some people find natural beekeeping hives more challenging to use and less productive in terms of honey, while others swear by the low-intervention, bee-centred approach. Ask four different beekeepers and you'll get five different answers. It's an interesting avenue to explore, however, not least because anything we can do to improve the number and natural vigour of honey bee populations has to be a good thing.

If you want to find out more about natural beekeeping, the Natural Beekeeping Trust is a fantastic place to start, and also has information about tree beekeeping and sun hives. The Barefoot Beekeeper also has an excellent website, with information including how to build your own natural beehive, where you can learn natural beekeeping, and ways to connect through an international forum that covers the US, UK, Ireland, Australia and New Zealand.

42

Adopt a Hive

———

If you haven't got time to keep bees, or don't have the space, it doesn't mean you can't be involved in beekeeping. An increasing number of people, and organisations, are adopting hives. Many of the national beekeeping groups run adoption schemes, which, in return for a yearly payment, give sponsors a window into the world of looking after bees. Depending on how involved you want to be, some of the schemes offer seasonal updates, jars of honey and bee information; others are more hands-on and encourage sponsors to visit the hives with a beekeeper or have a day's beekeeping experience.

Many organisations allow you to adopt a hive in a number of ways; you can either sponsor bees from a distance or, if you want to enjoy being up close and personal with honey production, some groups will partner with schools and communities, or even set up and manage a hive in your garden. They also encourage community groups to crowdfund beehives, whether you have a patch of common land to spare or a shared garden project.

Companies who are keen to improve their corporate social responsibility are also getting in on the act. Hotels, restaurants, retailers and other commercial ventures can adopt hives and, in return, not only get a boost to their sustainability credentials and free honey, but also know that their money is being used to provide free hives for charities and community projects that otherwise wouldn't be able to afford them.

Schools can also benefit from adopting a hive. In the US, Planet Bee Foundation allows schools to keep a hive on campus, maintained initially for two years by trained staff, but with the

long-term goal of letting the school take ownership of the colony. The organisation provides bee lessons for pupils, practical hands-on experience and the opportunity to harvest honey. The Honeybee Conservancy offers a similar 'Sponsor-A-Hive' scheme, which gives schools, community gardens and other local non-profit organisations a chance to connect with bees.

The idea of a practical, not just theoretical, approach to beekeeping in schools is one that can be tricky to get across to teachers and parents, but the benefits are profound. Looking after a colony not only lets pupils gain a working knowledge of beekeeping but also satisfies many different aspects of the curriculum – from biology and environmental science to food technology, history, design technology and art.

43

Save a Swarm

——

What do you do if you find a swarm of honey bees in your garden? While it can be scary to see a mass of tens of thousands of bees hanging off a tree branch or lamp post, swarming honey bees are actually at their gentlest. Before they leave the hive in search of a new home, the swarm will gorge itself on food for the arduous journey ahead – this makes them particularly docile and very unlikely to sting, unless provoked. Swarming honey bees are *not* the same as a nest of bees who have been disturbed – and this is where the confusion lies. Bees who are protecting their hive can be aggressive if their home is disturbed or damaged. People also mistake bees buzzing around the entrance to a nesting site or wild hive as a swarm – it's not, it's just the

busy comings and goings of an active colony.

A swarm of honey bees has no home or brood to protect, and so has no incentive to attack. Honey bees swarm in the spring and early summer, although it's not unknown for bees to swarm into a mild autumn. Bumblebees and solitary bees don't swarm.

If you see a cloud of bees, it's most likely a swarm in search of a new home. Don't disturb them or attempt to chase them away. They'll soon find somewhere to cluster. If a swarm has gathered on a post or tree in your garden, don't call the exterminator or pest control – your nearest beekeeper will be thrilled to come and collect the swarm for free, ready to take them to a new home. You can find a 'swarm collector' through your local Beekeepers' Association (see Directory, p. 125). Or contact your local council, who should have details of the local beekeepers' society.

It's not a good idea to try to collect a swarm if you don't know what you are doing – not only are you likely to get badly stung, but you'll end up doing more harm than good. There are also rare occasions when a swarm will act defensively – these are called 'dry swarms', who have used up their food stores and are starting to get hungry and irritable in their desperate search to find a new home. Also, if you see a cluster of honey bees but there's also honeycomb present, that's a nest, not a swarm.

44

Ditch Diesel

———

Diesel fumes have been shown to disrupt bees' ability to forage properly. Many car companies are ditching diesel in favour of cleaner alternatives such as electric or hybrid technology. Look into making the swap if you need to replace your vehicle or support local public transport systems that are fighting to tackle diesel pollution. London's long-term transport strategy, for example, includes new low-emission buses, zero-emission taxis and a zero-emission zone in central London.

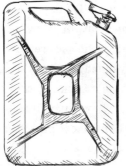

45

Know What to Do with a Bumblebee Nest

———

Unlike honey bees, which make those neat, hexagonal honeycomb homes we're all familiar with, the bumblebee nest is small and more informal. It's usually a clump of tiny golden or brown cells – rather like a mass of sugar puffs stuck together – beautiful but not particularly tidy. Some bumblebees nest underground, others in roof eaves, tree cavities and other cosy spaces such as compost heaps or under decking, so it's not difficult to stumble across one if you're gardening.

- The first thing to say is – DO NOTHING – bumblebees aren't aggressive. They also don't swarm, so the best course of action is just to leave them alone. The nest will only be busy for spring and summer, before being abandoned.

- If you disturb a nest by accident, it's best to simply stop what you're doing and let the bees repair any damage – if you try to cobble it back together or move it, you usually end up doing more harm than good.

- Beekeepers won't be able to relocate a nest of bumblebees but if a nest is causing real issues, you can find more information about rerouting a nest entrance at www.bumblebeeconservation.org or try the Tree Bee Society, who may be able to help.
- Don't panic if you find a bumblebee nest in a roof space or wall cavity – they won't cause any structural damage.
- If the nest is in an awkward place, wait until the end of the season (autumn) and block up the entrance so the queen can't use it again the following year.
- If you see a cloud of bumblebees flying around the entrance to a nest in summer – usually an old bird box or in the roof eaves – these are male bees eagerly awaiting the emergence of the new queen. They can't sting.

46

Teach Bee Whispering

———

One of the most important things to learn, and to teach others, is how to behave around bees. People, especially children, tend to panic if a bee flies close by, but wild flailing of hands and swatting at bees often makes the situation more risky.

- **Learn to stay calm near bees.** Bees are quick to sense movement and jerky or flapping motions may be interpreted as a threat – they'll soon lose interest if you appear 'invisible' by staying still. If you want to walk away, get up slowly and move calmly.

- **Understand what annoys bees.** They often interpret dark-coloured clothing as a threat (including red, which appears dark to bees). Wear light-coloured clothes when possible.

- The jury is out on whether wearing perfume and other scented products actively attracts bees. While it's probably best to **avoid wearing anything highly scented** if you're likely to be where there are lots of bees (that is, inspecting a hive), new research

suggests that bees who are exhibiting aggressive behaviour seem to calm down when they're exposed to floral scents such as lavender. This is because the bee thinks the scent is coming from a food source instead of a threat.

- **Remember that a bee doesn't want to sting you** – it's almost always a worse outcome for the bee. If a bee lands on you, stay still and let the bee fly away in its own time. Or you can very gently blow the bee away.

- Some beekeepers swear by the advice of **standing in the shade if bees are bothering you**. This is because bees are thought to prefer warmth.

- We really don't know whether bees are annoyed by loud voices, but **gently talking to a bee can help you stay calm**.

- **Notice bee behaviour** – if bees seem to be deliberately flying at your head or gathering in a group around you, they are probably trying to tell you there is a nest nearby.

- The only exception is if you have disturbed a nest and you are being deliberately targeted by a group of bees – in this instance, **protect your face and head if possible, and run** (indoors, ideally).

47

Bee First Aid

———

Bees are best left to their own devices, but there are three situations where human intervention can help. Learning a little 'first aid' could help rescue a bee in trouble – it might seem pointless, when a bee has such a limited lifespan, but each individual bee plays a vital role in the maintenance of the wider population.

HOW TO REVIVE AN EXHAUSTED BEE

You often find bees who have hit a spot of bad weather, struggled to find food, or are just exhausted from flying too far from the hive. Feeding them with a solution of pure white cane sugar and water will give them enough of an energy boost to get them back on their feet. (Sugar water should only be used as an emergency bee reviver, however, not an everyday source of food – it doesn't contain any of the important nutrients bees need.) The strength of the sugar water needs to vary, depending on the time of year.

- **SUMMER** – mix 3 teaspoons of water with 3 teaspoons of sugar.
- **AUTUMN** – mix 2 teaspoons of water with 3 teaspoons of sugar.

HOW TO RESCUE A DROWNING BEE

Bees need water (see 22. *Build a Bee Drinker*) and can get themselves into trouble if they venture too close to paddling pools, bird baths, ponds and swimming pools. They can be remarkably resilient, however, and even after a lengthy 'swim' can survive if they're gently rescued and left to dry out. Use anything flat (large leaf, hand trowel, plastic lid etc.) and lift the bee out from underneath. Leave the bee in full sun, where it can dry off and clean itself. You could also give it some sugar water as it's probably used its energy trying to stay afloat.

HOW TO GET A BEE OUT OF A HOUSE OR CAR

Don't try and waft a bee out of a confined space – bees see rapid arm movements as a threat (see 46. *Teach Bee Whispering*). Ideally, leave the window or door open and it should find its own way out. Failing that, cover the bee with a glass jar and wait for the bee to crawl up the side. Carefully slide a thin piece of card under the jar, taking care not to trap the bee's legs, and release the bee outside. If the bee won't come out, leave the jar outside until it does.

48

Take Part in a Bee Survey

Bee surveys – where members of the public record information from their local surroundings – are hugely helpful for a number of reasons. For a start, they help scientists get a better understanding of what's happening on the ground; the more people that take part, the bigger the sample size, the more reliable and useful the results. They also help researchers get a clearer idea of the scale of the problem, what kinds of numbers are involved, and what's happening among different bee species.

During Friends of the Earth's 'Great British Bee Count' in 2018, for example, nearly half a million bee sightings were submitted, from the Shetland Islands down to the Isles of Scilly, covering fifty different species. Similarly, in the US, the ongoing citizen science project 'Bumble Bee Watch' has gathered valuable information on native species across dozens of states, from Alaska to New Mexico.

The results from bee surveys not only help reverse the decline of bee populations but they also flag up interesting and unexpected data, not all bad. Sometimes a member of the public finds a rare species in an unusual location, for example, or a thriving bee population, or bee behaviours previously unrecorded by science.

Bee surveys also make you engage closely with your local environment in a way that you don't as a casual observer. Whether it's taking photos of bees on a smartphone or patiently counting the number of pollinators that visit your flower beds, actively watching and recording the behaviour of bees makes you look at nature through completely different eyes. Be warned, it's addictive once you start.

If you want to take part, the best place to start is to find out, online, which national bodies are organising a survey. Most are nationwide, so it doesn't matter where you live, and want data from both urban and rural settings.

Use the Directory (p. 125) at the back of the book to find a survey near you.

49

Bring Back Dark Skies

———

It's getting more difficult to find a genuinely dark night sky. We know that pollinating insects are affected by light pollution (see p. 10). Other animals are also disturbed by artificial light, from hedgehogs to wild birds – lighting up the night sky interrupts natural feeding patterns, migration and reproduction. It's a problem not just for wildlife, but also for human health: numerous studies have shown that exposure to artificial light at night – from street lamps to security lights – disrupts our bodies' ability to get to sleep.

A number of organisations are working hard to get the situation changed – the International Dark-Sky Association, and others like it, has been a long-standing voice in the fight against light pollution. Thanks to their work, the issue of light pollution is higher on the agenda and positive changes are being made: not only are cities across the world altering their lighting systems, but there's also a greater interest in dark skies festivals, star lore and 'astro-tourism'. Perhaps most importantly, they've drawn attention to scientific studies that show light pollution's destructive effects on night pollinators, nocturnal mammals and human well-being. So, what can we do to help?

- On a domestic scale, we can all reduce our reliance on outdoor lighting. Many of us keep a porch light or security lights switched on to feel safe, but the research suggests that there's little relationship between outdoor lighting and crime. Rather than have lights permanently on, **systems that detect motion are just as effective**. In fact, many local authorities are switching to 'adaptive street lighting', a larger-scale version of motion-detection technology.

- Ditch garden lights. The trend for night-time lighting in gardens has a measurable effect on wildlife. If you do buy outdoor lighting, generally speaking lights that **light only what you need, when you need it** will minimise pollution. Keep the brightness as low as possible and lights should point downwards, or be hooded, to reduce glare into the night sky. The International Dark-Sky Association has a list of approved fixtures that have been created to minimise light pollution.

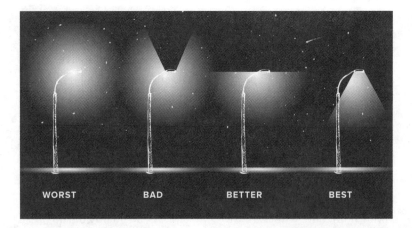

WORST   BAD   BETTER   BEST

- If you want to change your street lamps or intrusive commercial lighting, there are easy ways to **take action at a local level**. These include lobbying your local government, getting involved with planning, raising the issue with your representative, contacting local organizations and community groups, and working with schools (see Directory; p. 125).

50

Now You're Buzzing, Pass It On

Now you know what to do, become a bee champion. Raise awareness on social media. Spread what you've learned to friends and family. Give a talk to a local school or a community group. Share this book. **Bee inspired.**

BEE DIRECTORY

BEE-FRIENDLY SHOPPING

- USDA Organic (US) — *www.usda.gov/topics/organic*
- Canada Organic — *www.canada-organic.ca*
- Fair Trade (US) — *www.fairtradecertified.org*
- Bee Better Certified (Xerces Society, US) — *www.beebetter certified.org*
- Bee Friendly Food Alliance (US) — *www.environmentamerica .org/programs/ame/bee-friendly-food-alliance*
- Seeds of Diversity – Bee Friendly Farming (Canada) — *www .seeds.ca/pollination/bff-bfg*

BEEKEEPING ASSOCIATIONS, COURSES & FORUMS

- American Beekeeping Federation — *www.abfnet.org*
- American Bee Journal — *www.americanbeejournal.com/tiposlinks/ beekeeping-associations*
- Buzz About Bees — *www.buzzaboutbees.net*
- PerfectBee (US) — *www.perfectbee.com*
- Beekeeping Like a Girl — *www.beekeepinglikeagirl.com*

BEE CONSERVATION & RESEARCH

- National Bee Unit (DEFRA/APHA) — *www.nationalbeeunit.com*
- Bumble Bee Watch (US) — *www.bumblebeewatch.org*
- Xerces Society (US) — *www.xerces.org/bees*
- The Honeybee Conservancy (US) — *www.thehoneybeeconservancy.org*

- Pollinator Friendly Alliance (US) – *www.pollinatorfriendly.org*
- Save the Bees (Greenpeace) – *www.greenpeace.org/international/act/save-the-bees/*
- How to Bee Friendly (WWF) – *www.wwf.org.uk/updates/how-bee-friendly*
- Bees for Development – *www.beesfordevelopment.org*

NATURAL BEEKEEPING

- The Barefoot Beekeeper – *www.biobees.com*
- Bee Built (US) – *www.beebuilt.com*
- Gaia Bees (US) – *www.gaiabees.com*

PESTICIDES ACTION/POISONING

- Environmental Protection Agency (US) – *www.epa.gov/pollinator-protection/report-bee-kills*

PESTICIDE-FREE BULBS

- *www.organiccatalogue.com*
- *www.fruithillfarm.com*
- *www.groworganic.com*

COMMUNITY GARDENS & URBAN BEES

- American Community Gardening Association – *www.communitygarden.org*

BEE-FRIENDLY FARMING

- Bees Matter (Canada) – *www.beesmatter.ca*
- Farming for Bees (US) – *www.xerces.org/wp-content/ uploads/2008/11/farming_for_bees_guidelines_xerces_society.pdf*
- Farming for Pest Management (US) – *www.xerces.org/ wp-content/uploads/2008/09/farming_for_pest_management_ brochure_compressed.pdf*

ADOPT A HIVE / CHARITABLE GIVING

- Bees for Business – *www.beesforbusiness.com*
- Planet Bee Foundation – *www.planetbee.org*
- Adopt a Honeybee (WWF) – *gifts.worldwildlife.org/gift-center/ gifts/species-adoptions/honeybee.aspx*
- Remember a Charity – *www.rememberacharity.org.uk*

BEE HOMES

Bee Brick™ – *www.greenandblue.co.uk*

DARK SKIES

- The International Dark-Sky Association – *www.darksky.org*

GREEN ROOFS

- *www.wallbarn.com*
- *www.greenrooftechnology.com*

ABOUT THE AUTHOR

———

Sally Coulthard is a bestselling author whose titles include *The Little Book of Building Fires*, *The Little Book of Snow* and *The Hedgehog Handbook*. She also writes about rural life, craft and design. She lives in North Yorkshire.